The Toy Soldier

Elizabeth Gray - Virginia Evans

Express Publishing

Daddy: Here's a toy
for my little boy.
A toy soldier for you
And his jacket is blue!

William: Thank you, Daddy!
He's very nice –
He's got dark hair
And big brown eyes!

Daddy: And what have I got
For my little Rose?
A ballerina –
She can dance on her toes!

Rose: Thank you, Daddy!
She's beautiful, too!
She's got a pretty pink skirt
And pretty pink shoes!

Narrator: And now it is
            The end of the day.
            Time for the toys
            To come out and play.

Ted: Hello, I'm Ted.
            I'm a teddy bear.
            Look, my friends
            Are over there!
            That's Dolly, the doll
            And Jack in his box
            And Pip the puppet –
            One of William's socks!

Sam: I'm Sam, the toy soldier.
How do you do?
It's very nice
To meet all of you!

Bella: And my name's Bella.
Hello everyone!
I like it here,
It's lots of fun!

Sam: Follow me, follow me,
March if you can!
Swing your arms,
And count to ten!

One, two,
One, two, three!
Come on everyone,
Follow me! Follow me!

All: Hooray! Hooray!
It's the end of the day!
It's time for us
To come out and play!

Narrator: And now the day
Is here again!
The toys can't march,
Or count to ten.

Narrator: Now William and Rose
Are playing, you see –
But here comes Mummy,
It's time for tea!

Mummy: Time for tea!
Time for tea!
Come on! Come on!
Put your toys on the shelf
And run, run, run!

8

Narrator: Oh dear, poor Sam!
He's not on the shelf.
He's there by the window
All by himself!
It's windy today,
Look out! Look out!
Oh dear, poor Sam,
Can you hear him shout?

Sam:
Help me! Help me!
Help me, please!
I'm here outside
With the flowers and trees!
Where am I? Where am I?
Where are my friends?
Where's Bella? Where's Ted?
Oh, no! This is the end!

10

Ted: Come on, time to play,
I'm happy, I am!
But where's the toy soldier?
Where's our friend Sam?

11

Bella: Is he under the chair?
Is he there? Is he there?
Is he on the shelf
With the big teddy bear?
Oh, where is poor Sam?
Oh dear! Oh dear!
He's not over there,
He's not over here!

12

Narrator: It's sunny now,
The sky is blue,
But poor old Sam,
What can he do?
A big black dog
Comes running out,
And puts the toy soldier
In his mouth.

William: Oh Blackie, what's this?
Is it for me?
It's Sam, my toy soldier!
How can that be?
Thank you, dear Blackie,
Good boy! Good boy!
Now I can play
With my favourite toy!

14

Ted: Sam's here! Sam's here!
Everyone cheer.
Now all our friends
Are together again.
Let's dance and play –
Let's all shout HOORAY!

15

Bella: I like all the toys
In the children's playroom,
But my favourite toy,
Dear Sam, is you.

Sam: Dance with me Bella,
Round and round.
Come on everyone,
Let's all dance around.

The End

16

Picture Dictionary

Toys

toy soldier

ballerina

teddy bear

doll

puppet

jack-in-the-box

The body

dark hair

eyes

toes

arm

a mouth

Clothes

jacket

skirt

shoes

socks

Actions

dance

shout

march

run

play

Colours

pink

blue

brown

black

shelf

window

flowers

trees

Weather

It's windy.

It's sunny.

sky

18

Activities

1 Circle.

toy soldier

teddy bear

jack-in-the-box

puppet

doll

ballerina

2 Make your own toy soldier.
What's his name?

Hello, I'm ....

3 Read and colour.

I've got yellow hair
and green eyes.
I've got a red mouth.
I've got blue shoes.

4 Read and number.

JACKET: ....

SOCKS: ....

SKIRT: ....

SHOES: ....

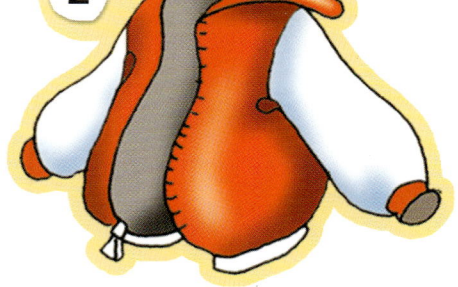

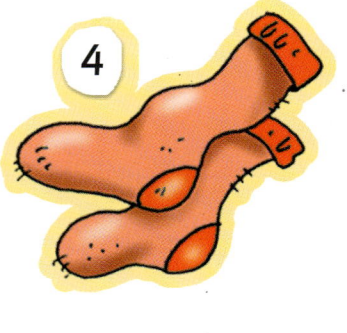

20

5 Look, read and complete.

s _ o _ t

d _ _ c _

m _ _ ch

6 Read and colour.

The sky is blue.
The sun is yellow.
The tree is green.
The flower is pink.

21

 **Circle the different weather.**

8 Draw you and your friend on a sunny day.

22

Express Publishing

Elizabeth Gray – Virginia Evans

The Toy Soldier

The Toy Soldier

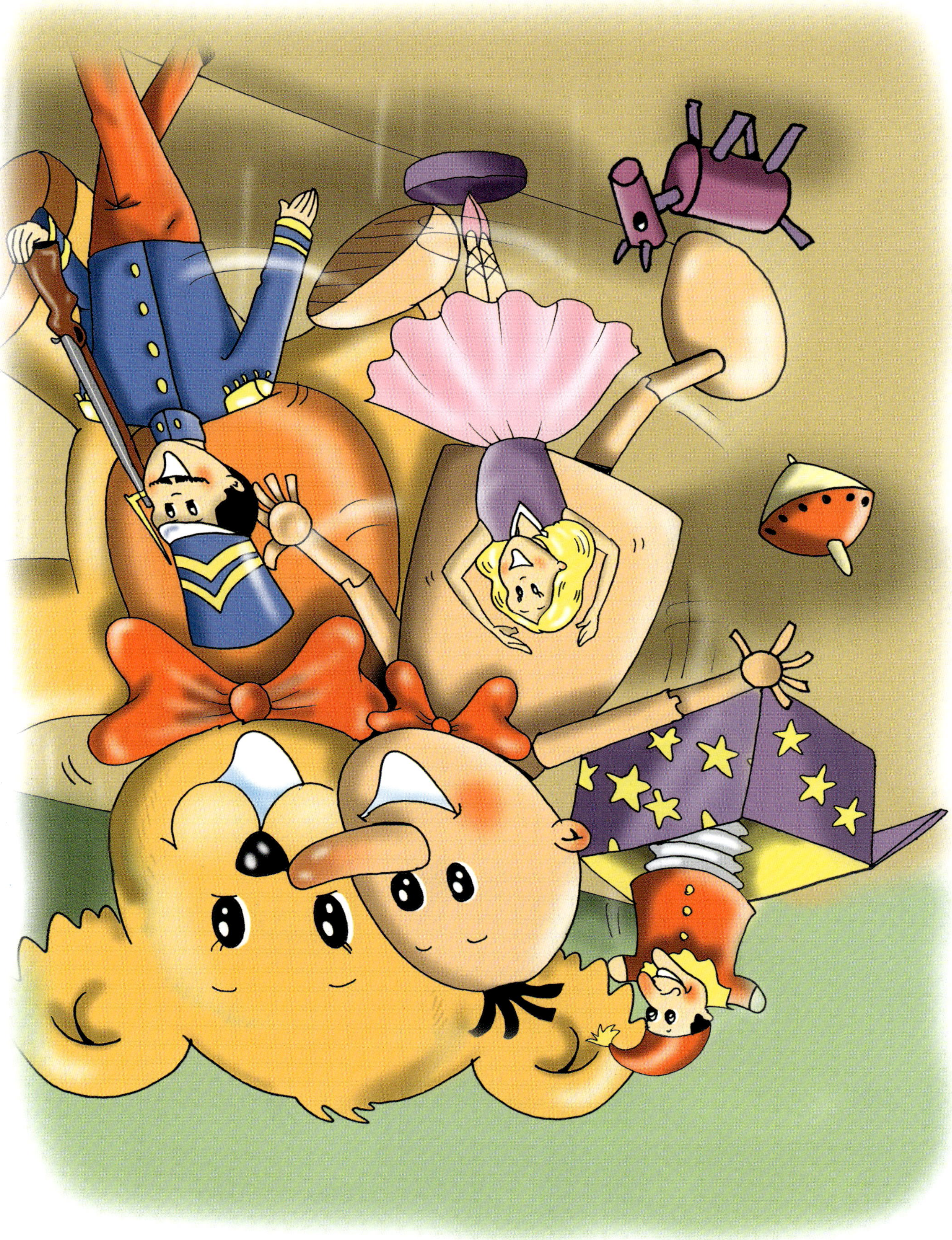

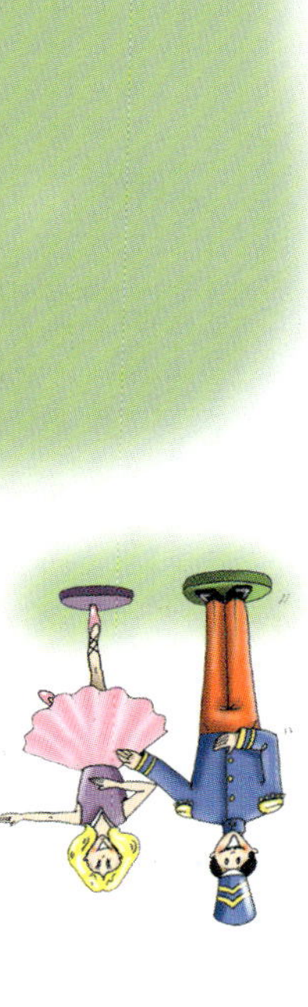

1 Match.

2. Help Sam go to Bella.